the beatitudes

Books by CHARLES L. ALLEN

ALL THINGS ARE POSSIBLE THROUGH PRAYER
GOD'S PSYCHIATRY
HEALING WORDS
IN QUEST OF GOD'S POWER
THE LIFE OF CHRIST
THE LORD'S PRAYER
PRAYER CHANGES THINGS
ROADS TO RADIANT LIVING
THE SERMON ON THE MOUNT
THE TEN COMMANDMENTS
THE TOUCH OF THE MASTER'S HAND
TWELVE WAYS TO SOLVE YOUR PROBLEM
THE TWENTY-THIRD PSALM
WHEN THE HEART IS HUNGRY
WHEN YOU LOSE A LOVED ONE
THE BEATITUDES

THE BEATITUDES

An Interpretation

CHARLES L. ALLEN

FLEMING H. REVELL COMPANY
OLD TAPPAN, NEW JERSEY

Illustrations by Ismar David

For

Kay DeMange Allen
who has blessed our family

Our Lord begins the Sermon on the Mount with the word "blessed." Some have translated the word as "happy," but Carlisle insisted that "blessed" is better—lest the word "happy" be confused with that vague something at which men grasp, and, grasping, miss. Jesus began by announcing, "I want to give you a happiness so deep, so lasting, so complete that you will be a blessed person."

Right at this point, we are in danger of missing the real purpose of the Christian faith. Christians have talked so much about sacrifice, about service, and about acceptance of the will of God that leads to a cross, that often we have missed the truth that Christ's purpose is to make people blessed. And how does this blessedness come to a life? Not by possessing something, nor by doing something, but rather in being something. Christ teaches us that true happiness comes as a result of certain qualities of character.

If you were to name the conditions under which you would be happiest, would you name the eight principles which make up the Beatitudes? If you possessed these eight qualities of character, would they make you a blessed person? Our Lord thought so, and before we reject His wisdom, let us seek to understand what He meant.

As a nation we have more to make life easy than any people who have ever lived. We live in the finest houses, wear the nicest clothes, and eat the best food that any generation has ever known. Yet, at the same time, we have more suicides, more divorces, more people in jail, more mental illnesses than any people throughout all of history. For numberless thousands of people, life is a grim, desperate, unhappy affair. In rejecting these basic principles of our Lord, we have also missed much of the real blessedness which life has to offer. We would do well to learn these principles at the feet of our Lord and put them into daily practice in our life.

When I think of happiness, two statements come quickly to my mind. One was from Albert Einstein. He said, "To make a goal of happiness has never appealed to me." The other statement is from the pen of Dr. Joseph Fort Newton: "If more people would get a divorce from themselves, they might live happily with someone else." Happiness is never something that we can seek directly; rather it is a by-product of a certain quality of life. As one forgets himself in seeking to be the person that our Lord pictures in the Beatitudes, he becomes a "blessed" person, which results in a deep and abiding happiness.

In this little volume I seek to suggest very briefly what I see as the meaning of each of these eternal principles.

CHARLES L. ALLEN

the Beatitudes

And he opened his mouth, and taught them, saying,

BLESSED ARE THE POOR IN SPIRIT: FOR THEIRS IS THE KINGDOM OF HEAVEN.

BLESSED ARE THEY THAT MOURN: FOR THEY SHALL BE COMFORTED.

BLESSED ARE THE MEEK: FOR THEY SHALL INHERIT THE EARTH.

BLESSED ARE THEY WHICH DO HUNGER AND THIRST AFTER RIGHTEOUSNESS: FOR THEY SHALL BE FILLED.

BLESSED ARE THE MERCIFUL: FOR THEY SHALL OBTAIN MERCY.

BLESSED ARE THE PURE IN HEART: FOR THEY SHALL SEE GOD.

BLESSED ARE THE PEACEMAKERS: FOR THEY SHALL BE CALLED THE CHIL-DREN OF GOD.

BLESSED ARE THEY WHICH ARE PERSE-CUTED FOR RIGHTEOUSNESS' SAKE: FOR THEIRS IS THE KINGDOM OF HEAVEN.

BLESSED ARE YE, WHEN MEN SHALL RE-VILE YOU, AND SHALL SAY ALL MAN-NER OF EVIL AGAINST YOU FALSELY, FOR MY SAKE.

REJOICE, AND BE EXCEEDING GLAD: FOR GREAT IS YOUR REWARD IN HEAVEN: FOR SO PERSECUTED THEY THE PROPHETS WHICH WERE BEFORE YOU.

MATTHEW 5:2-12

blessed are the poor in spirit: for theirs is the kingdom of heaven

M+5:3

FREDERICK WILLIAM IV of Prussia once visited a school and asked the children some questions. Pointing to the stone in his ring, a flower in his button-hole, and a bird that flew past the window, he asked to what kingdom each of them belonged. The children gave him the right answers: the mineral, the vegetable, and the animal kingdoms.

Then he asked, "To what kingdom do I belong?" That is really the supreme question facing every man. For some men the answer is the animal kingdom, because they live on the appetite level, and are controlled by their passions and physical desires. But most people rise above the animal level. They have a sense of right and wrong, a feeling of duty and decency, some ideals and purposes.

However, some rise to an even higher kingdom. No one can think of Christ as being animal. Though he took the form of man, the word "human" is insufficient to describe Him. Christ was divine. He belonged to a kingdom beyond the kingdoms of this world. The Bible tells us we can enter jointly with Him into His kingdom: "The Spirit itself beareth witness with our spirit, that we are the children of God: and if children, then heirs; heirs of God and joint-heirs with Christ" (ROMANS 8:16, 17).

We can belong to the Kingdom of God! That is a thrilling fact and gives to every life a thrilling mission. Recently someone asked me this question, "What do you want ten years from now?" I might answer that I want to be preaching, to be helping to build some church, some degree of comfort and security, to see my children becoming established in life. There are so many things I want.

But if I know my heart, as I think I do, I want, above all things, to belong to the Kingdom of God. Well, Jesus gave us eight keys to God's kingdom. The first key is poverty. Right off, we are tempted to say, "I qualify so far as poverty is concerned. Let's look at the second key."

But are you really poor? So far as material possessions are concerned, we are all poor. Even the man with a million dollars does not have enough to create one loaf of bread or to buy one moment of real contentment or to keep his soul out of hell. Yes, you are poor.

Also, the ten spies who went into the Promised Land were poor. Whimperingly they reported: "And there we saw giants . . . and we were in our own sight as grasshoppers" (NUMBERS 13:33). The man

with one talent was poor. He buried his talent in the ground. There are a lot of people who do not have the courage really to amount to anything. They are very poor, indeed.

On the other hand, one might possess a certain cocksureness and yet be very poor. Peter typifies that type of poverty when he says: "Though all men shall be offended because of thee, yet will I never be offended" (MATTHEW 26:33). He was not poor in spirit, yet he was poor, as it was proved when the testing time came.

The first key to God's Kingdom is another type of poverty.

Two men went up to the Temple to pray. One said, "God, I thank thee, that I am not as other men are." He listed all his good qualities and was quite satisfied. He had a good eye for himself, a bad eye for his fellow men, and no eye at all for God.

The other man prayed, "God be merciful to me a sinner." That man may have possessed great wealth, he may have had the courage of a conqueror, but he realized that he lacked something which only God could supply (LUKE 18:10,13). The poverty which is a key to God's Kingdom is the realization that, though we possess all things, without God all our things are nothing.

My favorite story is of a boy who had received money from his father, and had a spirit which made him feel he could conquer the world. In spite of his wealth and his spirit, however, he remained poor until one day he fully realized his real poverty, and said, "I will arise and go to my father" (LUKE 15:18). There is the poverty that makes rich—the realization of our lack of God and our desire for God.

"Blessed are the poor in spirit: for theirs is the kingdom of heaven." We sometimes interpret that word "blessed" to mean happy, but really it means a oneness with God. The "poor in spirit" have so emptied themselves of themselves—the pride of their accomplishments, the selfishness of their desires—that the Spirit of God has come into their emptiness. We sing, "What a joy divine, leaning on the everlasting arm"—that is it.

And what do we mean by the kingdom of heaven? Someone has said, "All that religion has to offer is self-denial in this life on the promise of some pie in the sky." But notice that Jesus uses the verb "is." His Kingdom becomes an immediate possession. It is not a place, it is an experience. It is not bounded by geographical lines, it is bounded only by our capacity to receive it.

Possessing the Kingdom, one possesses all things. The children of Israel were terrified. They had put their faith in Moses; he had died, and now they had lost everything. There are those of us today who put our faith in things which can die: rich one moment, we become poverty-stricken the next.

But not Joshua. Listen to his words to these fearful people: "Be strong and of a good courage; be not afraid, neither be thou dismayed; for the Lord thy God is with thee whithersoever thou goest" (JOSHUA 1:9). Joshua belonged in the kingdom of God.

Possessing God's power enables us to face life with enthusiasm; it gives us a deep inward peace because we are not afraid of tomorrow. There comes into our lives an inner joy that outward circumstances cannot reach. Because God is within us, and because God is love, there flows out from us a love for others that sweeps away all prejudice, jealousy, and hate.

In the light of the blessings of possessing the Kingdom of God, all our other possessions grow so dim that out of our very hearts we sing: "When other helpers fail, and comforts flee, help of the helpless, O abide with me."

BLESSED ARE THEY THAT MOURN: FOR THEY SHALL BE COMFORTED

M+ 5: 4

THE SECOND KEY to the kingdom of God is mourning. That is even less attractive to us than poverty, yet only those who can feel can mourn. There was Father Damien, for thirteen years a missionary to the lepers on Molokai. Finally the dread disease laid hold of him.

One morning he spilled some boiling water on his foot. But there was not the slightest pain. Then he knew he was doomed. He knew that death had come to his body and little by little would take possession. A hundred times better for him would it have been if that boiling water had brought pain.

St. Paul tells us of certain people who were "past feeling" (EPHESIANS 4:19). That is a horrible condition in which to be, yet, to some extent, each one of us is so afflicted. Socrates described a man's conscience as the wife from whom there is no divorce. Maybe we can't divorce our conscience, but we can stifle it until its voice is completely stilled.

A man whose feet were amputated told of his

experience. He was caught out in the bitter cold of the far north. So long as his feet pained him he was happy, but after a while the pain was gone, and he knew then that his feet were doomed. The pain diminished as they froze.

So with conscience. You have committed a certain wrong. Does it hurt? Then be glad. You become hopeless only when your soul becomes past feeling. Stuart N. Hutchinson tells of a small boy who, having been told by his father that conscience is a small voice which talks to us when we have done wrong, prayed, "O God, make the little voice loud."

"Blessed are they that mourn," said our Lord. He is not talking about the pessimist who constantly looks for the bad, nor of the selfish person whose ambitions have been thwarted, nor of the person who is bitter and rebellious over some loss. The first key to God's Kingdom, "poverty of spirit," tells us we should be conscious of our lack of God. Now, the second key tells us we should be so grieved over our moral and spiritual shortcomings that we cannot rest until we have found God, and our souls are satisfied.

Modern congregations have about discarded the old mourners' bench. It was a place where penitents came seeking divine pardon. In its stead we have a psychological clinic. Certainly I do not disparage the help of modern psychology. I have spent untold hours in counseling, but counseling by itself is not enough.

Today we want God's blessings without the pain of God's purging. We want sermons on how to win friends, how to have peace of mind, and how to forget our fears. But we must remember that Christ came to make men good rather than merely to make men feel good.

Often in my own church I have given people a chance to come and pray at the altar. Watching tears streaming down some praying face, I have felt like shouting for joy. The way of the Cross is not easy, but it is the way home.

Jesus told us, "And I, if I be lifted up from the earth, will draw all men unto me." Then the Gospel record adds, "This he said, signifying what death he should die" (JOHN 12:32,33). And as we see the suffering of the Saviour, surely it must bring suffering to us. Only a dead soul can see Him without mourning.

Let us remember that it is the sins of men that put Him there. If men had traveled less the paths of sin, His path up Calvary would have been less steep. If they had been less greedy and self-seeking, the nails in His hands would have burned less. If they had been less proud, his crown of thorns would have been less painful. If they had loved others more, they would have hated Him less.

On the cross He said, "Father, forgive them; for they know not what they do" (LUKE 23:34). Surely Pilate and Caiphas, Herod and the soldiers did not know what they were doing. Greedy, selfish men were merely putting out of the way one who got in their way. Their very ignorance helped Him to bear His cross.

But we do know. We have the record which has been taught to us from childhood. We are the ones who grieve Him most, who make the pain for Him the hardest to bear. He died to heal our broken hearts, and, instead, we break His heart by our own sin and our indifference to Him.

"Blessed are they that mourn." Those who care— care to the point of a broken spirit and a contrite heart, care to a deep repentance.

When Jesus came to Golgotha they hanged Him on
  a tree;
They drove great nails through hands and feet, and
  made a Calvary;
They crowned Him with a crown of thorns, red were
  His wounds and deep,
For those were crude and cruel days and human flesh
  was cheap.

When Jesus came to Birmingham, they simply passed
  Him by,
They never hurt a hair of Him, they only let Him die;
For men had grown more tender, and they would not
  give Him pain,
They only just passed down the street, and left Him
  in the rain.

(From "The Unutterable Beauty" by G. A. Studdert Kennedy, published by Hodder & Stoughton, Ltd.)

Maybe you are afraid. You dread to come into His presence. You are ashamed to face Him. You may feel miserable inside. Then take heart and be glad, for your very shame and misery and fear are a mourning that can lead you to His comfort.

As you look at your life you may see your own broken heart. Be glad that it is broken. Take it to Calvary. There, under the warm glow of His love, your broken heart can be welded together again, and your sorrow be turned into rejoicing. Be thankful for your broken heart, if by becoming broken we are led to Christ for the mending.

blessed are the meek: Mt 5:5
for they shall inherit
the earth

ONE OF the keys to the kingdom of God is meekness.
But we do not want to be meek. We prefer to be
like the little boy whose mother kept calling him,
"My little lamb." Finally, he said, "Mother, I don't
want to be your little lamb. I want to be your little
tiger."

We like to think of ourselves as being courageous
and strong. We sing with inspiration, "The Son of
God goes forth to war, a kingly crown to gain," but
meekness does not appeal to us. We want to be
conquerors, and meekness sounds too much like
surrender. Meekness does mean surrender, but not
surrender to men around us, not surrender to ourselves, not surrender to the circumstances of our
lives.

For the true meaning of meekness turn to the
Thirty-seventh Psalm. There you find it stated, "The
meek shall inherit the earth." The Hebrew word
which is translated "meek" really means "to be
molded." The Psalmist says, "Fret not thyself because

of evil-doers," do not be envious of the prosperity of the wicked. Instead, "Commit thy way unto the Lord." That is, let yourself become as putty in God's hand, be molded by Him, yield your life to the purposes of God, and eventually real success will be your reward.

Jesus lifted up that phrase of the Psalmist and made it one of the Beatitudes, a key to God's Kingdom. The New Testament writers used the Greek word *praos,* which we translate as "meek." Actually, it means to be controlled. It means submission to the divine plan of God.

The laws of God are already established when we are born. His ways are fixed. We have a choice in that we can accept God's way and live according to His law, or we can rebel against Him. But we cannot change what He has done. For example, the world is round and the sky is blue. Suppose you don't like round worlds and blue skies. There is nothing you can do about it.

Also did God make the laws of the universe, which are just as unchangeable as is the universe itself. There are the seasons. The farmer learns the laws of the seasons and becomes governed by them. He plants his crop when it should be planted and thus he reaps when he should be reaping. For him to rebel and plant out of season does not change the laws of God, it means only the failure of his crop. For the farmer meekness means planting when he should plant. It means submission to God's laws.

So with life. God has His will, and man has his will. Man has the choice of being meek or of being self-willed. He can say with Christ, "Nevertheless, not my will, but thine, be done" (LUKE 22:42), or man can say, "I will do as I please." The Psalmist says, "Delight thyself also in the Lord; and he shall give thee the desires of thine heart" (PSALM 37:4). On the other hand, to fail to become molded or controlled by God's will is to destroy ourselves.

In the last chapter of the book of Job is a thrilling statement. Job's life had both sunshine and shadows. He had his successes and also his defeats. He had faith in God, yet there were times of doubt. It seemed that Job might "curse God," as he was advised to do. But in the end his faith triumphs and Job says, "I know that thou canst do everything" (42:2).

There are times when, with our limited vision, it seems that God's way is not the best way. We want material success on earth, we want happiness in our lives and peace in our hearts. If we believed, really believed, God would give us what we so much want; we would gladly be meek, that is, be willing to be molded and controlled by God. But it wasn't until he became an old man that Job knew without doubt that God is never defeated.

How wonderful it is to learn that lesson while there is still much of life to be lived. One of the sublimest statements outside the Bible comes from Dante, "In

His will is our peace." The opposite of peace is conflict and the reason we do not have peace of mind and soul is that we are at war within ourselves.

There is the voice of duty and there is the voice of inclination, both within us demanding to be heard. We struggle to decide, and the struggle squanders our powers. We become weakened and exhausted. But when one decides to do the will of God, day by day, as best he understands it, the conflict is resolved.

Such a decision takes all of the dread out of tomorrow. The wise man of the Bible tells us, "In all thy ways acknowledge him, and he shall direct thy paths" (PROVERBS 3:6). The very act of accepting the will of God for your life today places the responsibility of what happens tomorrow on God. So we do not worry about what the result will be. There is wonderful peace in leaving the results in His hands. An old Negro man once prayed, "When God tells me to butt my head against a rock wall it's my place to butt. It's the Lord's place to go through." As you study the lives of God-molded people down through the centuries you realize that every time God did "go through." In the long run, God is never defeated.

I think of how Mahatma Gandhi left Sabarmati on March 12, 1930, to go on the "salt march." He proposed to march to the sea, there make salt, which was a government monopoly, and thus precipitate a crisis. He said he would not return until he had gained independence for India.

It seemed absurd. A little man in a loin cloth and with a bamboo walking stick going out to do battle against the greatest empire the world had ever known. But seventeen years later the little man had won. Gandhi's power lay in the fact that his life was committed to the will of God as he understood it. Thus committed, he was totally without fear. And his freedom from fear struck fear into the heart of the British Empire and it dared not destroy him.

"Blessed are the meek," said Jesus. Those who surrender to God possess God. We are told, "The earth is the Lord's and the fulness thereof" (PSALM 24:1). Thus, possessing God, the meek do also "inherit the earth."

BLessed ARe they which do hunger and thirst after Righteousness: for they shall be filled

ONCE A young man came to Buddha seeking the true way of life, the path of deliverance. According to the story as Dr. Ralph Sockman tells it, Buddha led him down to the river. The young man assumed that he was to undergo some ritual of purification, some type of baptismal service.

They walked out into the river for some distance and suddenly Buddha grabbed the man and held his head under the water. Finally, in a last gasp, the fellow wrenched himself loose, and his head came above the water. Quietly Buddha asked him, "When you thought you were drowning, what did you desire most?" The man gasped, "Air." Back came Buddha's reply, "When you want salvation as much as you wanted air, then you will get it."

Jesus would agree with that. He tells us that one of the keys to the Kingdom of God is to hunger and thirst for it. We get what we really want. The poet Shelley pointed out that imagination is the great instrument of moral good. When the imagination and the will are in conflict the imagination always wins.

To imagine is to form mental images on the screens of our minds. It means to create in our thinking what we want created in our living. One's time, talents, and all other resources become organized and dedicated to the purpose of making real the objects of his imagination. As Georgia Harkness said, "Be careful what you set your heart on, for you will surely get it."

Jesus tells us that before we can possess God and the things of God we must first make God the center of our imagination. "Thou shalt love the Lord thy God with all thy heart, and with all thy soul, and with all thy mind" (MATTHEW 22:37), said Christ. And when God becomes the very center of our affection, our feeling, and our thinking, we shall find and possess and be possessed by God.

The greatest thrill this preacher ever has is to see some person attain a deeper experience of God. Every Sunday night, as I see hundreds pray at the altar of the church, I know that some are finding God there. But long before time for the altar prayers I can almost pick out those who will be blessed that night.

Watch a congregation during the organ prelude and you will see a lot of difference. Some are quiet in thought and prayer. They seem hardly conscious of their immediate surroundings. Others are chatting away with everyone around, they watch others as they come in, note their clothes, and wonder about them.

When the hymn is announced, some sing not only with their voices but also with their hearts. Others just say the words or don't even bother to pick up the hymnbook. During the sermon some are like blotters. They soak up every thought and mood of the preacher. Others seem utterly unresponsive.

What makes the difference? Some have needs that human resources do not supply. They have come to church feeling that need, hungering and thirsting for God, and it is they who find Him. You never find God until He becomes your deepest desire.

Two men were discussing New York City. One said it was a wicked place, filled with cheap sensations, with morally degraded people, with sin on every corner. The other said it is a grand place, filled with art museums, great music, and stimulating lectures. New York was the city that each inwardly desired.

We find in life what we want to find. So Jesus said, "Blessed are they which do hunger and thirst after righteousness: for they shall be filled."

It bothers me that the church seems to mean so little to many of its members, that in the church so many find almost no help. It is not the church, it is our own attitudes. Once a rather pious churchman was reproving his neighbor for profanity. The profane neighbor replied, "Well, my friend, I cuss a lot and you pray a lot, but neither of us really means what he says."

In one of his books Bishop Fulton J. Sheen says,

"It is not uncommon to find Catholics who say: 'I knew I should not eat meat on Friday out of respect for the day on which Our Lord sacrificed His life for me, but I did not want to embarrass my host,' or, 'I was staying with some unbelieving friends over the week end and I did not want to embarrass them, so I did not go to Mass on Sunday'. . . . Such is the indifference of the world, a fear of being identified whole-heartedly with God, for whom we were made."

What he says of Catholics is, perhaps, even more true of Protestants. If we really desire God we will do those things which will cause us to experience God. Jesus says that we should hunger and thirst after God. I saw a picture show recently of a man lost on the hot sands of a desert, without water. His thirst whipped his weary body to the point of madness. His distorted mind was mocked with a cruel mirage of an oasis. He died frantically digging with his bare hands in the sand.

"Thirst" is a strong word, a driving word. And when the human soul thirsts for God, Jesus says he will be filled with God. And not only will we find God for ourselves, we will bring God's Kingdom on earth.

Just suppose that there was only one real believer on earth and that during an entire year this one believer made one convert. Then there would be two. Suppose that during the next year these two made one convert apiece, then there would be four. Suppose that the next year these four made one convert apiece, then there would be eight. Suppose that they kept that pace of each winning one every year, how long would it take to convert every person in the entire world?

It has now been two thousand years since our Lord was on earth. Has that been enough time? Actually, there has been time enough, with just one winning one other per year, to convert sixty-five worlds like this. Starting with just one and doubling each year, at the end of just thirty-one years there would be 2,147,483,648 souls filled with God's righteousness. The next year they could convert another world the size of this one.

We can have God in our souls and in our world whenever we really want Him.

BLESSEÒ ARE the meRCiful:
foR they shall
oBtain meRcy

OF THE eight Beatitudes, the keys to God's kingdom, this one is the most appealing, the most important, and the most difficult. Most appealing because
mercy brings to mind kindness, unselfish service, and
good will. Everyone loves the Good Samaritan and
Florence Nightingale, who are examples of mercy.
We shrink from the justice of God, but we pray for
His mercy.

Most important, for without mercy all of us are
without hope. All of us have sinned and come short
of God's glory. The only prayer we can pray is,
"God be merciful to me a sinner" (LUKE 18:13). As
Portia said to Shylock, "In the course of justice none
of us should see salvation."

When we come to the Communion table we pray,
"We are not worthy so much as to gather up the
crumbs under Thy table. But Thou art the same
Lord whose property is always to have mercy." However, the key to God's mercy toward ourselves is the
mercy we have toward others. If we are not merciful,

37

then we are blocking God's mercy out of our own lives, and thus we become doomed men and women.

There is a saying, "All that goes up must come down," but if nothing goes up, then nothing will come down. In physics we are taught that every action has a reaction, but if there is no action, then there can be no reaction. "If ye forgive not men their trespasses, neither will your Father forgive your trespasses" (MATTHEW 6:15). Without forgiving, forgiveness cannot be obtained. Be merciful, and ye shall obtain mercy.

The most expensive thing you can do is hold a wrong spirit in your heart against another. The price you pay is the loss, the eternal loss, of your own soul. In talking about the Kingdom of Heaven Jesus tells the story of a king who forgave his servant a large debt which he could not pay. That same servant met a fellow servant who owed him a trifling sum, and because he could not pay, the poor fellow was thrown into prison by the unmerciful servant. The king called back the servant whom he had forgiven, cancelled his forgiveness, and had him cast into prison.

Jesus concludes the story, "So likewise shall my heavenly Father do also unto you, if ye from your hearts forgive not every one his brother their trespasses" (MATTHEW 18:23-35).

Protestants do not regard Peter as the head of the Church as do Catholics, yet beautiful is the explanation a Catholic friend gave to me of why he believes

Peter was chosen. James and John asked for the chief places, but they were passed by, as was the Virgin Mother, or one of the others. Peter was chosen because he sinned so shamefully but later wept so bitterly. Tradition tells us that Peter wept so much that even his cheeks became furrowed with tears.

So the Lord chose him who knew by experience the blessing of merciful forgiveness in order that his life should cause the Church to put at its very center mercy toward others, thereby saving itself as it saved others. Without being merciful, no one can enter the Kingdom of God. Not only is this key the most appealing and important, also it is the most difficult. When someone has done us wrong our natural human reaction is to seek revenge, to get even. We might refuse to commit any definite act of vengeance, yet cherish resentment and be glad if some misfortune happened to him.

Mercy requires not only a right spirit on our part against a person who has wronged us, not only that we must overcome all vindictiveness, jealousy, and littleness, but that we must do even more than feel a kind spirit in our hearts. Jesus wept, but He did more than weep. He gave Himself even unto death to serve and save those who had persecuted Him.

In his book *High Wind At Noon* Allan Knight Chalmers gives us the story of Peer Holm, who was a world-famous engineer. He built great bridges, railroads and tunnels in many parts of the earth; he gained wealth and fame, but later came to failure, poverty, and sickness. He returned to the little village where he was born and, together with his wife and little girl, eked out a meager living.

Peer Holm had a neighbor who owned a fierce dog. Peer warned him that the dog was dangerous, but the old man contemptuously replied, "Hold your tongue, you cursed pauper." One day Peer Holm came home to find the dog at the throat of his little girl. He tore the dog away, but the dog's teeth had gone too deeply and the little girl was dead.

The sheriff shot the dog, and the neighbors were bitter against his owner. When sowing time came they refused to sell him any grain. His fields were plowed but bare. He could neither beg, borrow, nor buy seed. Whenever he walked down the road, the people of the village sneered at him. But not Peer Holm. He could not sleep at night for thinking of his neighbor.

Very early one morning he rose, went to his shed, and got his last half bushel of barley. He climbed the fence and sowed his neighbor's field. The fields themselves told the story. When the seeds came up, it was revealed what Peer had done, because part of his own field remained bare while the field of his neighbor was green.

Mercy requires that we sow good seed in our enemy's field, even though it means that part of our own field will be left bare. It is not easy. It is the hardest possible action, but it is our key to God's Kingdom.

The way of the world was an eye for an eye and a tooth for a tooth. Hate always led to hate. Wrong always brought revenge. But one day the vicious circle was broken. One called Jesus came offering men a higher way and a better life, but men stood back to mock and to laugh and to crucify.

About His head was a bright circle, and when He uttered the word, "Forgive," that circle of God's love and approval became large enough to include others. A thief on a cross near by stepped inside that circle with Him and in so doing entered Paradise. The circle reaches to my own feet. To stay outside is to know hate, revenge, and destruction. Inside is to know God's healing love and eternally to possess His Kingdom.

The step into the circle is the step to mercy. "Blessed are the merciful: for they shall obtain mercy."

BLESSED ARE THE PURE IN heart: for they shall see god
M+5:8

THERE ARE many things I would like to see—the Grand Canyon, some of the great cathedrals of Europe, the paths in the Holy Land along which the Saviour walked. I want to continue to see my home happy and peaceful, I want to see my children growing mentally and spiritually as well as physically, and some day become established in some useful work in the world. I want to see always the difference between right and wrong. Most of all, I want to see God.

But all people have not the same ability to see. Many people have limited vision. Some are cross-eyed, the eyes of some are weak and diseased. Some people have a defect called a cataract, which shuts off vision. Some are near-sighted, others, far-sighted; some are color-blind, others have blind spots in their eyes. Sidney Lanier looked at the muddy crooked Chattahoochee river and saw in it a lovely poem; Joel Chandler Harris saw in rabbits, foxes, 'possums, and an old man named Uncle Remus, stories which will

43

live forever. Woodrow Wilson could see a basis of lasting world peace, but tragically so few others saw it. Sir Christopher Wren could see a beautiful cathedral and make of that vision a temple to God.

There are at least three ways in which we see. St. Paul tells us that "eye hath not seen, nor ear heard, neither have entered into the heart of man, the things which God hath prepared for them that love him" (I CORINTHIANS 2:9). There we have pointed out three kinds of sight. There is the sight of the natural eye, with which we can see flowers and mountains, the printed words on this page, and people's faces. That is physical vision.

A teacher may explain to a boy a problem in mathematics or chemistry. As the teacher talks, the boy hears, and his mind takes hold of what he hears to the point of understanding. After he understands, he might say, "I see it." That is mental sight. In studying botany a student can reach the point of learning the various kinds of flowers and of their culture and development. Then he can see flowers with both his physical and mental eyes. If one understands what he reads, he sees with both his eyes and his mind.

But there is still a third sight, as when a truth has "entered into the heart of man." The heart has eyes, too. Robert Burns saw in flowers thoughts too deep for tears. Not only did he see flowers with his physical eyes, not only did he understand the growth and culture of flowers, also he felt their message. Jesus looked at people and had "compassion on them."

He saw them not only with His eyes and mind, but also with His heart. One can read the Twenty-third Psalm and understand the meaning of the words and phrases. But some read it and they feel the message and know the Good Shepherd. A boy can look at a girl and know that he loves her. He sees her not only with his eyes but with his heart.

A person sees God through the eyes of the heart. "Blessed are the pure in heart: for they shall see God" (MATTHEW 5:8). Jesus said: "He that hath seen me hath seen the Father" (JOHN 14:9). Certainly not every person who saw Him with his physical eyes saw God. Mere physical sight of Him revealed only a man. It is not even enough to understand His teachings and His life. Many scholars have studied His words without seeing Him. Really to see God in Christ one must experience Him in the heart.

What a wonderful change in my life has been
  wrought,
Since Jesus came into my heart.
I have light in my soul for which long I have sought,
Since Jesus came into my heart.

When the heart sees Christ, then we see God. To see God is to realize Him, to feel Him, to center the affections of the heart in Him.

But one can have an indistinct and distorted picture of God. Read the story, "The Quest for the Holy

Grail." The holy grail was the mystic cup used at the Last Supper, in which legend has it that Joseph of Arimathea caught the last drop of blood which fell from our Lord's side as He died on the cross. Sir Galahad, along with other Knights of the Round Table, set out in quest of it. In the story they found it, but each saw it through the mirror of his own soul.

To some it was swathed in mist and cloud. Their vision was very indistinct. Sir Lancelot saw it, but his heart was a sinful heart. He saw the holy grail covered with holy wrath and fire. To him it was a vision of stern and awful retribution. Sir Galahad also saw the grail. He was the knight with the white soul. Of him it was said, "His strength was the strength of ten because his heart was pure." For him the vision was clear and radiant and glorious.

How we see God depends on the condition of our hearts. To some He is a cloudy mystery, to others He is awful punishment, but to the pure in heart He is a friend and a glorious certainty.

Suppose one has lost purity of heart, can it be regained? Can a harlot become a virgin again? Yes, St. Augustine refers to Mary Magdalene as "the arch-virgin." Not content to call her merely a pure woman, he lifts her far above other women. She was a common prostitute of the streets. She was both vile and vulgar. But one day she came in contact with Him who was the purest. She so loved Him with her heart that all her affection was poured out on Him. She so completely took Him to heart that her evil desires were cast out. Being filled with the purity of Christ, she herself became pure.

In just a little while we see her standing at the foot of Jesus' cross. See who is by her side! It is Mary, the Lord's mother, the blessed Virgin. The two are standing together. Purity has been regained. Paradise lost has now been regained. And on Easter morning Mary Magdalene became the first vessel chosen by Christ Himself in which to send forth the blessed Gospel. If Mary Magdalene could become pure again, then there is hope for every one of us. She saw Christ with her heart.

"Blessed are the pure in heart: for they shall see God."

blessed are the peacemakers: for they shall be called the children of god

WHAT DO we want most of all? Whenever I am in the vicinity of Warm Springs, I like to stop by the little cottage which Franklin D. Roosevelt loved so much. There he would come to rest and to think in the quietness of that lovely place. The night before he died he was there planning a trip to San Francisco to attend the organization of the United Nations. He was writing his speech—the last words he ever wrote. They were:

We seek peace—enduring peace. . . . We must cultivate the science of human relations—the ability of all peoples, of all kinds, to live together and work together, in the same world, at peace. . . . As we go forward toward the greatest contribution that any generation of human beings can make in the world— the contribution of lasting peace—I ask you to keep up your faith.

Above all things, peace was the desire of his heart, as it is of my heart and of yours. We want peace in our world—we want peace inside ourselves. The fact that the late Rabbi Joshua Loth Liebman's book *Peace of Mind* has now sold nearly a million copies is eloquent testimony that people are interested in peace.

The angel climaxed the announcement of the birth of our Lord with the words, "Glory to God in the highest, and on earth peace, good will toward men" (LUKE 2:14). Peace was His mission. "Peace I leave with you, my peace I give unto you" (JOHN 14:27). When we think of the Kingdom of God, we think of a kingdom of peace, where all strife has ceased. So we are not surprised that our Lord gave peace as one of the keys to the Kingdom.

As Rabbi Liebman pointed out at the beginning of his book, there are many earthly things we desire—health, love, riches, beauty, talent, power, fame; but without peace of mind all those things bring torment instead of joy. If we have peace, no matter what else we may lack, life is worth living. Without peace, though we may possess all things else, it is not enough.

What is peace? The mere absence of strife is not peace. At the moment Jesus was speaking of peace there was no war on earth, but neither was there peace. The Roman Empire had forced the world to its knees and the people had lost both the means and the will to fight. When Paris surrendered to German fury without struggle, someone said, "London lost her buildings, but Paris lost her soul."

Peace is a positive force. You may clear some plot of land of every noxious weed, but that will not make of it a garden. It will be only a barren field. It becomes a garden when flowers are growing there. The prophet of old reminds us that just to break up our swords and spears is not enough. Those swords must become plowshares and the spears pruning hooks (MICAH 4:3).

To have peace in both the world and our souls, not only must hate, suspicion and fear be rooted out. Also must love, joy, patience and understanding be planted and cultivated. Peace is something to be made; thus we must be peacemakers if we are to enter the kingdom of God.

The place to begin making peace is within ourselves. Dr. Ralph W. Sockman in his book, *The Higher Happiness,* which is the most helpful book on the Beatitudes I know, lifts up the words of Christ, "And if a house be divided against itself, that house cannot stand" (MARK 3:25). Then he points out three ways by which a life is divided: between its inner self and its outer self, between its forward drive and its backward pull, between its higher and lower natures. Let's look at these a moment.

INNER AND OUTER SELVES

The Pharisees became chiefly concerned with keeping up a front. All of their actions were "to be seen of men." They were worried about what neighbors would think. Seeking to appear to be something outside which they were not inside, they became hypocrites. A hypocrite is one without peace. Unless our outward appearances and our inward character are in harmony with each other, we have no peace.

FORWARD AND BACKWARD

Physically, we are made to go forward. To walk backward is awkward. A little girl was trying to button her dress in the back. Finally, she gave up and went to her mother for help, saying, "I can't do it because I am in front of myself." But mentally we are just the opposite. We can think better backward than forward. We know what happened yesterday, we can only guess about tomorrow. Thus it is easier to live in the past, and reluctantly we turn it loose.

We load ourselves down with futile regrets and mistakes of yesterday; thus the business of living becomes a hard pull. Instead of repentance, we know only the meaning of remorse. Remorse is futile worry and self-inflicted agony for some yesterday. Repentance is a redemptive experience which leads to forgiveness. It buries the past under the hope of tomorrow.

HIGHER AND LOWER NATURES

Finally, we make peace by the decisions of our souls. Elijah stood before the people on Mount

Carmel and pleaded, "How long halt ye between two opinions? If the Lord be God, follow him: but if Baal, then follow him." He was pleading for a decision. The Bible says, "And the people answered him not a word" (1 KINGS 18:21). Oh, the tragedy of one who cannot make a decision. There is marvelous inner peace which comes to one who completely decides for God. I suppose there is a peace, certainly a cessation of inner strife, which comes to one who decides against God. But to go through life undecided is to live in misery. "No man can serve two masters." Two thousand years ago Jesus said that, yet we have not learned it.

The oldest story of man tells how he sinned and then hid himself from God. Hiding from God is the most miserable experience the human soul can experience. Peace with God is the most blessed experience. One of the greatest thinkers of all time was Copernicus. He revolutionized the thinking of mankind in regard to the universe. The epitaph on his grave at Frauenburg is this: "I do not seek a kindness equal to that given to Paul; nor do I ask the grace granted to Peter; but that forgiveness which thou didst give to the robber—that I earnestly pray." That is the way to begin making peace.

The angel said, "Glory to God," before he said, "Peace on earth."

BLESSED ARE THEY WHICH ARE PERSECUTED FOR RIGHTEOUSNESS' SAKE: FOR THEIRS IS THE KINGDOM OF HEAVEN

Mt 5:10

THE SERMON on the Mount recorded in Matthew 5, 6, and 7 is really the pattern of the Kingdom of God on earth. Jesus begins that sermon with the listing of the eight keys to that kingdom, the qualities of character of the Godly person. The climax of the Beatitudes and the sermon are really one and the same.

In the sermon He tells us how to live, and He concludes with a call to action, the expression of those principles in daily living. "Whosoever heareth these sayings of mine, *and doeth them,*" He says. At the beginning of the sermon He lists the qualities of character, as poverty of spirit, mourning, meekness, desire for righteousness, mercy, purity of heart, and peacemaking. Then He says, "Blessed are they which are persecuted." That is, actually to live these keys to the kingdom will cost something. But unless they are translated into life they are worthless.

Jesus never promised ease to those who follow Him. Never did He put a carpet on the race track or a bed of roses on the battlefield. He talked about self-denial, about crosses, blood-spattered, death-dealing crosses. To enter the Kingdom of God may mean decisions that are hard, consecration that leads to persecution. But it can be no other way.

In Revelation, St. John writes to the Christians, "Fear none of those things which thou shalt suffer: behold, the devil shall cast some of you into prison, that ye may be tried; and ye shall have tribulation ten days [indefinitely]: be thou faithful unto death, and I will give thee a crown of life" (2:10). Notice carefully one little word there. He does not say "until" death, but "unto" death. That means, be faithful, not merely until you die, but even though it kills you. Make whatever sacrifice is required, even die, before you be unfaithful.

A minister friend tells of going to a large church to preach at a special Good Friday night service. The weather was extremely bad and only a few people came. Apologetically, the pastor said to the visiting minister, "If it had not been for the bad weather we would have had a large crowd to hear you tonight."

At first, it angered the visiting minister, but quickly his anger turned to pity and contempt. Looking at his host, he said, "Do you realize what you have just said? If the weather had not been bad a larger crowd would have come to this Good Friday service. Jesus

died on Good Friday, but His followers did not come to the service because the weather was bad."

When I started in the ministry I did not have a car. Sometimes I would walk to my little churches, sometimes I would borrow the horse and buggy of an old physician, Dr. George Burnett. One very cold and rainy Sunday morning I said to the doctor that I would not go to the little church out in the country because I doubted that anyone would be there. He looked at me with contempt. I will never forget the sternness of his voice. He said, "It is your duty to be there. Get the horse and go."

No person ever really lives until he has found something worth dying for. You can never really possess the Kingdom of God until the cause of God becomes more important than your own life.

William L. Stidger told about a young lad he had baptized as a baby. The boy grew up, and when World War II began, he joined the Navy. One night his ship came into Boston, and the lad visited his former pastor and friend. During their visit together, Dr. Stidger said, "Bill, tell me the most exciting experience you have had thus far." The boy seemed to hesitate. It wasn't that he had difficulty in selecting the most exciting experience. Rather, the experience he had in mind was so wonderful and sacred that he had difficulty in putting it into words.

He was the captain of a large transport and, along with a big convoy, was making his way across the

Atlantic. One day an enemy submarine rose in the sea close by. He saw the white mark of the torpedo coming directly toward his transport, loaded with hundreds of boys. He had no time to change course. Through the loud-speaker he shouted, "Boys, this is it!"

Near by was a little escorting destroyer. The captain of that destroyer also saw the submarine and the torpedo. Without a moment's hesitation, he gave the order, "Full speed ahead." Into the path of the torpedo the tiny destroyer went and took the full impact of the deadly missile midship. The destroyer was blown apart, quickly it sank, and every man of the crew was lost.

For a long time the boy remained silent. Then he looked at his beloved pastor and said, "Dr. Stidger, the skipper of that destroyer was my best friend." Again he was quiet for a while, then slowly he said: "You know there is a verse in the Bible which has special meaning for me now. It is, "Greater love hath no man than this, that a man lay down his life for his friends" (JOHN 15:13).

> *The Son of God goes forth to war,*
> *A kingly crown to gain.*
> *His blood-red banner streams afar;*
> *Who follows in His train?*

To be poor in spirit means to give up our pride; to

mourn means to be penitent to the point of surrendering our sins; meekness means that we must surrender our very selves to the plans and purposes of God; our hunger for God means turning away from our ambitions for all things else; to be merciful means to pay good for the evil we have received; for purity we must give up all things impure; to make peace is wholly to choose God. Those are the seven ingredients of righteousness. They must be bought at a price. Blessed are those who pay the price, "for theirs is the kingdom of God."